The Rapture

Biblical Proof Theologians Have Missed

ERIKA GREY

Pedante Press

Short Book Series

008

All Scriptural quotations in this publication are from the New King James Version of the Bible © by Thomas Nelson, Inc.

DEDICATION

To all those inquiring about the promise to
every believer living in these end times

CONTENTS

www.erikagrey.com

For Bible Prophecy news and analysis and more books visit my website. For Bible Prophecy Updates on video subscribe to my Podcast and YouTube channel Prophecy Talk with
Erika Grey.

1
THE RAPTURE

The Tribulation is a seven-year period of God's horrific judgments onto the earth. It is marked by wars, plagues, famines, earthquakes, and catastrophic, apocalyptic events in nature. These are detailed in the book of Revelation along with supporting passages in many other books of the Bible, It ends in the Battle of Armageddon, and the Second Coming of the Lord Jesus Christ.

Part of the earth's judgments happen through a frightening world leader referred to as the Antichrist. Not only is he responsible for a great deal of bloodshed and war, but he makes people on the earth take his mark. Those who do not take the Mark of the Beast will be murdered. The details of the Tribulation are so horrifying that the hope that many cling to is the teaching of the Rapture.

The Rapture

The Rapture is a term that Evangelical Christians have given to the precept that those who are redeemed by the blood of Jesus will not go through the seven-year period of judgements described in the book of Revelation. Therefore, they will be taken out of the earth, just before the Tribulation begins and meet the Lord in the sky. Those living prior to the Rapture will have lived through the fulfillment of the end time signs with all the hardship they bring. The book of Daniel refers to this time as the transgressors coming to the full, meaning that society is marked by grievous sinful, immoral behavior.

Five Views of the Rapture

Despite the doctrine, not all theologians and prophecy students agree on the teachings regarding the Rapture. According to Manfred E. Kober, TH.D of Faith Baptist Theological Seminary, there are five Rapture positions. From the partial Rapture adherents who believes only those who are watching will be raptured, to the mid Tribulation view that the Rapture will occur during the middle of the Tribulation. The Pre-Wrath Rapture regards it as occurring during the fourth quarter of the earth's final seven years. These are among the views that Manfred Kober mentions.

The other belief is the Post Tribulation Rapture. This teaches that there is no Rapture and only the second coming of the Lord Jesus Christ. Many Calvinists hold this idea. Therefore, Evangelical Christians are divided on their interpretation of the Rapture Scriptures.

In short some believe the Rapture occurs after the Tribulation. Others believe it happens before the Tribulation begins and some that it never takes place. The view that I will prove in this work, is the Pre-Tribulation Rapture or Pre- Trib view that the Rapture occurs just prior to the start of the seven-year Tribulation.

The Pre -Trib Rapture Teaching's Origins

The word Rapture is not used in the Bible. It is a term and doctrine first noted and taught by British theologian, educator and Bible translator John Nelson Darby. He who lived from 1800 to 1882, in around 1830. Darby is the father of dispensationalism. In his day he was the leading interpreter of Bible Prophecy. John Nelson Darby was a leading figure of the Plymouth Brethren, which originated in Dublin, Ireland. Christian Historians credit him as the originator of the Rapture promise and the father of modern dispensationalism and futurism.

The Teaching Spread

Darby taught that Christ will suddenly remove His bride, the Church. The belief was popularized by publisher Dwight Moody who also founded the Moody Bible Institute in 1886. During one of his visits to England in the 1870's he met Plymouth Brethren, who informed him of the Rapture doctrine. That same year Moody invited Scofield to address a biblical conference in Northfield, Massachusetts. The focus was the authority of Scripture, acceptance of Jesus Christ as savior, and the period of earthly tribulation preceding the Second Coming.

In 1890 Scofield established the Central American Mission and in 1895 a correspondence Bible course that enrolled 10k students' intent on being pastors. In 1905 he went to work on his reference Bible, which was published in 1909. In 1913 Scofield helped found Philadelphia School of the Bible, which later became Cairn University. He died in 1921. During his life was instrumental in bringing the Pre–Tribulation Rapture doctrine into the mainstream of Biblical teachings via his Bible Colleges, churches, and publications.

Yet not all theologians agreed and thus came the varying views. In this work, I will not bore you with theologian's jargon or who teaches which idea, rather this book omits all the non-essential information and instead proves the Rapture from pure analysis of the Scriptures. Moreover, it highlights teachings and passages untouched by these theologians.

Lack of Study

The varying perspectives result in great part to a lack of research of the writings in the Bible. Even schools of theology teach what has been put together by former educators. In Bible Prophecy are cliches that have been handed down since the early 1900's, that are not applicable, such as one world religion. The late

Jimmy DeYoung of Prophecy Today who was part of Word of Life and was a great contributor to Bible Prophecy News at a certain point stopped doing the research and was repeating fake new and popular conspiracy theories. When it came to the European Union his information was literally fiction. He even adopted Covid vaccine conspiracies which believe it is government control. DeYoung died of COVID-19 at the age of 81. The media jumped on the fact that a religious broadcaster who endorsed COVID-19 conspiracies died of COVID-19. His story presents a good example of lack of research in end time prophecy.

Distinct Settings

Jesus clearly describes two distinct and diverse settings of His return in the Rapture vs. the Second Coming. Moreover, other passages during the Tribulation are disregarded that also prove the Rapture. These will be discussed in this work. It becomes clear that the Bible provides evidence of a Pre-Tribulation Rapture, which this book will reveal, minus the theology speak. I challenge any non-Rapture theologian or student to refute the Scriptural proof provided in these pages.

2

NO PLAGUES FOR THE SAINTS

The righteous do not suffer God's earthly judgements. God ushered Lot and his family out of Sodom and Gomorrah before destroying the city. He commanded Noah to build the ark, rescuing his kin from the flood. We see a pattern in the Old Testament that God does not let his people go through the judgements reserved for the unbelieving wicked. God brings those who have placed their faith in his Son during the Church dispensation out of the Tribulation

Ezekiel 9

In line with the righteous not suffering God's

judgements we read about those who were spared in Ezekiel 9. In this account God decreed judgement on Jerusalem because the people descended into grievous sin and immorality. God sent six angels to destroy the sinful inhabitants and to not spare any of them. But, before God sent this plague of death, he instructed the angels to mark the righteous by putting a mark on their foreheads. This is also like the mark received by the 144 thousand, more on this in a later chapter.

Ezekiel 9: 3-4 calls the man clothed in linen who had an inkhorn to mark the righteous. Many believe this is Jesus: *"Now the glory of the God of Israel had gone up from the cherub, where it had been, to the threshold of the temple. And he called to the man clothed with linen, who had the writer's inkhorn at his side,*

Ezekiel 9:5 describes the judgment that took place, it reads:

"To the others He said in my hearing "Go after him through the city and kill; do not let your eye spare, nor have pity. Utterly slay old and young men, maidens and little children and women; but do not come near anyone on whom is the mark; and begin in my sanctuary." And the Lord said to him, "Go through the midst of

the city, through the midst of Jerusalem, and put a mark on the foreheads of the men who sign and cry over all the abominations that are done within it.

The Tribulation Saints

It seems a contradiction that there are believers during the Tribulation who will go through it, when God's pattern is to spare the righteous his wrath. We call these believers the Tribulation Saints and they are saved in the final dispensation.

The Final Dispensation

The earth's last seven years is the final dispensation of God working in the land of Israel and among the Jews. The book of Daniel announces 70 weeks of specific prophetic events which will affect the nation, Israel. A Biblical week equals seven secular years. Seventy biblical weeks total 490 years, which encompass three decrees affecting Jerusalem. Two of these have already happened: from the edict to rebuild Jerusalem under Cyrus, down to the cutting off the Messiah, was 483 years. The remaining seven years await fulfillment (Dan. 9:24).

Christians in the Tribulation

Simultaneous with the Rapture is the sealing of the 144 thousand Jewish witnesses. They get saved just after the Rapture. For more on the 144 thousand witnesses see my book on them. These will in part act as Evangelists who will preach during the Tribulation. These will be among those martyred. Therefore, the Tribulation Saints are primarily the Jewish believers in God's final seven years dealing with the nation of Israel.

Division of Righteous and Unrighteous

God miraculously ends the Ezekiel 38 war, which is a major miracle and sign from Him. This gives cause for the Antichrist to initiate the peace treaty, which God refers to as the Covenant of Death. There will then be the division of righteous and unrighteous Jews based on those who embrace the Antichrist as Messiah and those with wisdom and understanding who know his identity and have accepted Christ.

Grace Does Not End with Rapture

The Rapture ends the Gentile church age.

Grace does not end. Those who take the Mark of the Beast will lose their salvation, because the Mark blasphemes the Holy Spirit. Jesus warned of the unpardonable sin during His ministry. Only it was not possible for men to commit the sin during that era. So, there is no contradiction or inconsistency. Moreover, the Holy Spirit is at work and does not leave when the Church is taken out in the Rapture. Evangelicals taught this falsehood without realizing that the Holy Spirit is at work during the Tribulation. It is in the Tribulation that the unforgivable sin can be committed via the Antichrist. For more on this see my book Decoding 666 the Number of the Beast.

The Martyrs Will Not Suffer the Plagues

Revelation 12 states that during the time of the persecution by the Antichrist, the 1260 days, that God has a place prepared for the believers in the wilderness. Moreover Revelation 12:6 adds that in the course of the 1260 days of their persecution they are fed by God. It states:

6 Then the woman fled into the wilderness, where she has a place prepared by God, that they should feed her there one thousand two hundred and sixty days.

Therefore, the Tribulation Saints do not suffer the third seal from the famine predicted in Revelation 6: 5-6:

5 When He opened the third seal, I heard the third living creature say, "Come and see." So I looked, and behold, a black horse, and he who sat on it had a pair of scales in his hand. 6 And I heard a voice in the midst of the four living creatures saying, "A quart of wheat for a denarius, and three quarts of barley for a denarius; and do not harm the oil and the wine."

The Bible also mentions Tribulation Saint's protection from the fifth trumpet. These are the releasing of the locusts from the bottomless pit that sting men for five months. Revelation 9: 4-6 states:

4 They were commanded not to harm the grass of the earth, or any green thing, or any tree, but only those men who do not have the seal of God on their foreheads. 5 And they were not given authority to kill them, but to torment them for five months. Their torment was like the torment of a scorpion when it strikes a man. 6 In those days men will seek death and will not find it; they will desire to die, and death will flee from them.

Just as in Ezekiel 9, these believers marked by God to not experience the plagues.

All of the Tribulation Saints Will Die

While the Tribulation Saints are shielded from the Revelation Plagues, and the worst occur after their deaths, they are not exempt from the Antichrist's campaign to kill them. The Bible tells us that the Antichrist accomplishes his aims, and each Christian is murdered. Moreover, this proves that there is no Rapture at the end of the Tribulation because there are no living believers on the earth when Jesus returns.

God Will Not Destroy the Earth if One Righteous Person Were Left

This aligns with what God promised to Abraham that if there was one righteous person left in the cities, God would not destroy them. This was relayed in God's conversation with Abraham when he asked God if there were ten righteous would He destroy the cities of Sodom and Gomorrah and God told Abraham no.

In line with God's judgements not effecting the righteous, the worst of the Revelation plagues; the seventh trumpet, which issues the bowl judgements are unleashed onto the earth after their deaths While there will be the martyrs during the Tribulation who will die under the campaign of the Antichrist, the worst of God's plagues are reserved for after the last Saint is killed. There is not one Christian left at the pummeling of the earth by the stars and the great earthquake that levels mountains and sinks islands around the globe. Therefore, the Rapture fits in line with God's pattern and the martyring of the Tribulation Saints do not defy it.

3

1ST RESURRECTION BRANCHES INTO THREE

One of the Scriptural facts that theologians have missed is that there are three resurrections that are part of the First Resurrection. The Second Resurrection happens after the millennium. The First Resurrection comprises of Jesus raising believer's bodies on three separate occasions. Each aligns with a dispensation. Revelation 20:4-6 names this teaching.

Three Resurrections Aligns With Three Days

The first divides like a fractal into three separate resurgences of the physical bodies of believers. This corresponds with the three days from Jesus's death until His resurrection. Some confusion in the Rapture verses arise over the failure to recognize the triad within this teaching. Often people will call these contradictions when on the contrary they are the Scriptural doors to deeper truths.

The Raising of the Old Testament Saints

We see the first of the three in Matthew 27:36 51-53:

Then, behold the veil of the temple was torn in two from top to bottom; and the earth quaked, and the rocks were split, and the graves were opened; and many bodies of the saints who had fallen asleep were raised; and coming out of the graves after His resurrection, they went into the holy city and appeared to many.

The first resurrection was of the Old Testament Saints and any who died while Jesus walked the earth.

The Second of the Three Resurrections

The second resurrection of believers occurs at the Rapture. These are Christians who were saved during the church age. There will be both a bringing to new life of those who died during the church age as well as the Christians who are alive.

1 Corinthians 15: 51-52 promises:

Behold, I shew you a mystery; We shall not all sleep, but we shall be changed, In a moment, in the twinkling of an eye, at the last trump; for the trumpet shall sound, and the dead shall be raised incorruptible, and we shall be changed.

'We shall not all sleep" indicates those that are alive when the Rapture occurs, which does not fit either the first or the third of the three resurrections.

At Jesus' Second Coming is the Third Resurrection

The third and final resurrection happens at the Second Coming. This is the resuscitation of the bodies of the Tribulation Saints who were martyred. Matthew 24:29-31 confirms:

29 "Immediately after the tribulation of those days the sun will be darkened, and the moon will not give its light; the stars will fall from heaven, and the powers of the heavens will be shaken. 30 Then the sign of the Son of Man will appear in heaven, and then all the tribes of the earth will mourn, and they will see the Son of Man coming on the clouds of heaven with power and great glory. 31 And He will send His angels with a great sound of a trumpet, and they will gather together His elect from the four winds, from one end of heaven to the other.

Another reason for Jesus's appearance at His Second Coming is to resurrect and gather the remains of those who died during the Tribulation. These are the bodies of the Tribulation Saints to be reunited with their spirits. Revelation 6:9 records that the souls of the Tribulation Saints are seen under the alter. They have not yet received their resurrected bodies.

Jesus is the Resurrection

Without Jesus there is no resurrection of the Saints. He stated in John 11:25, *"I am the resurrection and the life; the one believing in Me, even if he should die, he will live.* "Jesus being the resurrection is confirmed by the First Resurrection of Saints. This is literally true as we see in Scripture as He is present at each event. He comes for each of our remains to revive them on the last day of our dispensation.

God's Pattern-The Fractal

In my book Decoding 666 I talked about God's pattern being a fractal pattern that branches out and continues. This is best revealed in the chief God symbol the tree. Whereas the main Satanic symbol is the circle because it is confined and does not give to life but to death. We also see a fractal pattern in the issuance of the seal, trumpet and bowl judgements that flow from and into each other. The eco system acts as a giant fractal as do the events in our lives. Jesus said in John 15:5, *"I am the vine and you are the branches."* Again, a fractal pattern in the three resurrections that make up the first resurrection. Thus, the First Resurrection branches into three. The basis of the Rapture is that it is the second part of the First Resurrection.

Three Days Three Dispensations

One of the reasons for the three days until Jesus's resurrection is each day represents the last day for each dispensation for the bodies of His elect to be gathered. These events are sounded by trumpets and assisted by angels. Simultaneously in the Earth are major earthquakes. When Jesus died on the cross at the exact time of his death was a great earthquake and the graves opened. At the Rapture simultaneously with the earthquake of Ezekiel 38-more on this in a later chapter- the Rapture occurs. The bodies of those who have died will be rejoined with their spirits. Those who are still alive will change in the air. It should be noted that when the two witnesses resurrect, there is also an earthquake. We see in God's throne room in Revelation 4:5, lightning and thunder and quakes. Lightening is an electrical charge and thunder is the sound the strike makes. So we see that when God works forces in nature including earthquakes accompany His actions.

4

LIFTED UP VS. RIDING A HORSE

In line with the various dispensations, we also see the return of Jesus described differently for each of them. When you understand the three resurrections, you can see which applies. For instance, Acts 1:9-11 fits the arrival of Jesus in the Rapture.

Acts 1:9-11 describes:

And when he had said these things, as they were looking on, he was lifted up, and a cloud took him out of their sight. And while they were gazing into heaven as he went, behold, two men stood by them in white robes, and said, "Men of Galilee, why do you stand looking into heaven? This Jesus, who was taken up from you into heaven, will come in the same way as you saw him go into heaven."

This is not what is depicted in the Second Coming. Revelation 19: 11-14 describes Jesus riding a horse.

11 Now I saw heaven opened, and behold, a white horse. And He who sat on him was called Faithful and True, and in righteousness He judges and makes war. 12 His eyes were like a flame of fire, and on His head were many crowns. He had a name written that no one knew except Himself. 13 He was clothed with a robe dipped in blood, and His name is called The Word of God. 14 And the armies in heaven, clothed in fine linen, white and clean, followed Him on white horses.

Gathered to The Lord

This contrasts 2 Thessalonians 2:1, which states, *"Concerning the coming of our Lord Jesus Christ and our being gathered to Him, we ask you, brothers and sisters."* Being gathered to the Lord contrasts the Saints who accompany and follow Him on white horses.

Meeting the Lord in the air aligns with 1 Thessalonians 4:17, which states, *"Then we who are alive and remain shall be caught up together with them in the clouds to meet the Lord in the air. So shall we ever be with the Lord.* It becomes apparent, that there are two appearances of Jesus, one at the Rapture. Moreover, the word used in the phrase for "caught up together with them in the clouds" means to catch away, to seize, carry off by force, to snatch out or away. This does not at all match the picture of the Saints riding horses with Jesus at the Second Coming.

There are some who regard Matthew 24:28 and Jesus's statement that "Wherever there is a carcass, there the vultures will gather" as also pertaining to the Rapture. There are differing views on the meaning and for those who adhere to the idea that this is another Rapture verse, it provides another example of the illustration of gathering vs. riding behind Jesus on horses.   Moreover, it disproves a Rapture at the end of the Tribulation of those who are alive, because there is not one Christian living at the end of the Tribulation.   More on this in a later chapter.

5

THEIF VS VICTORIOUS KING

. Over the next several chapters we will be examining the Rapture passage found in Matthew 24:36 to 44. First, we will look at Jesus coming as a thief. The passage reads:

36 "But of that day and hour no one knows, not even the angels of heaven, but My Father only. 37 But as the days of Noah were, so also will the coming of the Son of Man be. 38 For as in the days before the flood, they were eating and drinking, marrying and giving in marriage, until the day that Noah entered the ark, 39 and did not know until the flood came and took them all away, so also will the coming of the Son of Man be.

40 Then two men will be in the field: one will be taken and the other left. 41 Two women will be grinding at the mill: one will be taken and the other left. 42

Watch therefore, for you do not know what hour your Lord is coming. 43 But know this, that if the master of the house had known what hour the thief would come, he would have watched and not allowed his house to be broken into. 44 Therefore you also be ready, for the Son of Man is coming at an hour you do not expect.

It is clear that at the Second Coming Jesus does not come as a thief but for all to see. Yet in this verse clearly, He likens Himself to a robber. This means undetected, and as a thief comes in hidden and at a time they are not expecting.

This contrasts Matthrew 24:30:

30 And then shall appear the sign of the Son of man in heaven: and then shall all the tribes of the earth mourn, and they shall see the Son of man coming in the clouds of heaven with power and great glory. Revelation 1:7 adds: *'Behold, He is coming with clouds, and every eye will see Him, even they who pierced Him. And all the tribes of the earth will mourn because of Him. Even so, Amen. "*

The Third Resurrection of the First

Matthew 24 talks about both the Second Coming and the Rapture in one passage. It also references the third and final resurrection of the bodies of the Tribulation Saints.

Matthew 24:31 describes:

31 And he shall send his angels with a great sound of a trumpet, and they shall gather together his elect from the four winds, from one end of heaven to the other.

On the thief references, Jesus also signifies that to those who are not watching for Him, he will appear to come as a thief. His appearing is unexpected by those believers who are not following Him, and by the unbelievers on the Earth at the time of the end. The thief references number seven, with four relating to the Rapture and three to the time of the end.

The Thief Verses

These references are as follows:

1 Thessalonians 5:2 SECOND COMING
For you yourselves know full well that the day of the Lord will come just like a thief in the night.

1 Thessalonians 5:4 RAPTURE
But you, brethren, are not in darkness, that the day would overtake you like a thief.

2 Peter 3:10 SECOND COMING

But the day of the Lord will come like a thief, in which the heavens will pass away with a roar and the elements will be destroyed with intense heat, and the earth and its works will be burned up.

Revelation 3:3 RAPTURE

So remember what you have received and heard; and keep it, and repent. Therefore if you do not wake up, I will come like a thief, and you will not know at what hour I will come to you.

Revelation 16:15 SECOND COMING

("Behold, I am coming like a thief. Blessed is the one who stays awake and keeps his clothes, so that he will not walk about naked and men will not see his shame.")

Matthew 24:43-RAPTURE

But be sure of this, that if the head of the house had known at what time of the night the thief was coming, he would have been on the alert and would not have allowed his house to be broken into.

Luke 12:39-RAPTURE

"But be sure of this, that if the head of the house had known at what hour the thief was coming, he would not have allowed his house to be broken into.

Jesus comes as a thief at the time of the end because the last thing the wicked will expect is His appearing. At the Rapture He comes unexpectedly with no specific time frame given but the season and takes those out of the world that are His.

6
IN FIELD VS CLEFTS OF ROCKS

There is another contrast in the Bible of the Rapture and the Second Coming that show two very different times. Matthew 24:40-41 records a relatively normal period when two men are in a field, and two women working and in each case one is taken and the other left.

Matthew 24:40-41 records:

40 Then two men will be in the field: one will be taken and the other left. 41 Two women will be grinding at the mill: one will be taken and the other left.

Whereas at the Second Coming, men are hiding in caves and in the rocks of the mountains. There is also no mention of one being left behind in these rocks, rather they are hiding in them. The women grinding at the mill are working a normal workday.

Luke 17:34 adds: *"I tell you, in that night there will be two in one bed. One will be taken and the other left."* These are sleeping calmly and not hiding.

Revelation 6:15-17 confirms:

15 And the kings of the earth, the great men, the rich men, the commanders, the mighty men, every slave and every free man, hid themselves in the caves and in the rocks of the mountains, 16 and said to the mountains and rocks, 'Fall on us and hide us from the face of Him who sits on the throne and from the wrath of the Lamb! 17 For the great day of His wrath has come, and who is able to stand?"

Great Earthquake and Hail

In addition, at the time of the Second Coming is the big earthquake with great hail.

Revelation 16:17-21 confirms:

17 Then the seventh angel poured out his bowl into the air, and a loud voice came out of the temple of heaven, from the throne, saying, "It is done!" 18 And there were noises and thundering's and lightnings; and there was a great earthquake, such a mighty and great earthquake as had not occurred since men were on the earth. 19 Now the great city was divided into three parts, and the cities of the nation's fell. And great Babylon was remembered before God, to give her the cup of the wine of the fierceness of His wrath. 20 Then every island fled away, and the mountains were not found. 21 And great hail from heaven fell upon men, each hailstone about the weight of a talent. Men blasphemed God because of the plague of the hail, since that plague was exceedingly great.

Two Contrasting Periods

Therefore, we see two contrasting periods in addition to Jesus acting as a thief and coming unexpectedly. Moreover, by taking one and leaving the other behind during normal routines, the thief not only appears unexpectedly but takes something out of the world. This is another area where Biblical sceptics would say that the Bible is full of contradictions, rather it is another area of deeper truths revealed. As you can see there are no incongruities in Scripture.

7
DAY OR HOUR VS NO. OF DAYS

Often when talking about the signs of the times many will say that no one can know the day or the hour. This certainly regards the Rapture and is talking about its timing. Although one can know the season in which it will occur. Jesus relayed this in talking about the leaves on a fig tree. But in contrast the Tribulation Saints are given the number of days of their lives, along with the timing of God's final judgements onto the earth.

Revelation 13:14 states of the woman, which is Israel in the wilderness during the persecution during the Tribulation period, *"But the woman was given two wings of a great eagle, that she might fly into the wilderness to her place, where she is nourished for a time and times and half a time, from the presence of the serpent.* It is this time frame that the martyrs are being killed and their murders are completed at the 1260th day. This is three and a half years. It marks the second half of the final seven years of the 490 predicted by Jeremiah the prophet regarding the nation of Israel.

How can a Rapture Occur When no Christians Are Alive?

The Bible makes it very clear that there will not be one Christian alive at the time of the end Therefore how can a Rapture occur at the end? Moreover, if there are no Christians at the time of the end how can the verse that states *We shall not all sleep, but shall be changed in a moment, in the twinkling of an eye* occur as foretold in 1 Corinthians 15:51-52.

God Makes it Clear all Christians Will Die During the Tribulation

As God was giving the prophet Daniel the end time visions and their interpretation, the prophet Daniel asked when the fulfillment of these things would occur? Jesus, who is speaking in Daniel 12 confirmed, *"when the power of the holy people has been completely shattered, all these things shall be finished.*" This lines with Daniel 8:24, which predicts of the Antichrist that *"He shall destroy the mighty and also the holy people."*

Antichrist Shall Prevail Against Saints

Daniel 7: 25 adds that God allows the Antichrist to persecute the Saints.

He shall speak pompous words against the Most High, Shall persecute the saints of the Most High, And shall intend to change times and law. Then the saints shall be given into his hand For a time and times and half a time.

Daniel 7:21 includes, *I was watching; and the same horn was making war against the saints and prevailing against them.* The next verse is noteworthy, *"until the Ancient of Days came and a judgement was made in favor of the saints of the Most High, and the time came for the saints to possess the kingdom* (this occurs with the destruction of the earth and the return of Christ.) We see this theme repeated further down in Daniel 7:26-27, indicating that the end of this king's reign is the end of the world. Daniel 8:12 further confirms, *"he did all this and prospered."*

The Bible relays the death of the martyrs in Revelation 12:11: *And they overcame him by the blood of the Lamb and by the word of their testimony, and they did not love their lives to the death.*

The Bible describes in Revelation 6:9-12 that each of the martyrs is given a white robe. They are slain "for the word of God and the testimony which they held.

Those With Wisdom and Understanding

We see a particular theme in the book of Daniel and the Revelation of the righteous during the Tribulation referenced as having wisdom and understanding. Revelation 13:18 states, *"Here is wisdom. Let him who has understanding calculate the number of the beast, for it is the number of a man: His number is 666."* Daniel 11: 35 corresponds:" And *some of those of understanding, shall fall to refine them, purify them and make them white until the time of the end.*

Daniel 12:9-10 adds, *and some of those of understanding"* and *"none of the wicked shall understand but the wise shall understand"*

These have understanding and wisdom and for this reason do not take the Mark of the

Beast and they pay with their lives.

God's Talk With Abraham

In part God allows the martyrdom of Christians in the Tribulation because the final judgements cannot be released with them on the Earth. When God was going to destroy Sodom and Gomorrah, Abraham prayed for the cities. God let it be known that He would not destroy them if there were any righteous in them. Moreover, neither will He destroy the world if one righteous person remains. Genesis 18:22-33 records:

22 Then the men turned away from there and went toward Sodom, but Abraham still stood before the Lord. 23 And Abraham came near and said, "Would You also destroy the righteous with the wicked? 24 Suppose there were fifty righteous within the city; would You also destroy the place and not spare it for the fifty righteous that were in it? 25 Far be it from You to do such a thing as this, to slay the righteous with the wicked, so that the righteous should be as the wicked; far be it from You! Shall not the Judge of all the earth do right?"

26 So the Lord said, "If I find in Sodom fifty righteous within the city, then I will spare all the place for their sakes."

27 Then Abraham answered and said, "Indeed now, I who am but dust and ashes have taken it upon myself to speak to the Lord: 28 Suppose there were five less than the fifty righteous; would You destroy all of the city for lack of five?"

So He said, "If I find there forty-five, I will not destroy it."

29 And he spoke to Him yet again and said, "Suppose there should be forty found there?"

So He said, "I will not do it for the sake of forty."

30 Then he said, "Let not the Lord be angry, and I will speak: Suppose thirty should be found there?"

So He said, "I will not do it if I find thirty there."

31 And he said, "Indeed now, I have taken it upon myself to speak to the Lord: Suppose twenty should be found there?"

So He said, "I will not destroy it for the sake of twenty."

32 Then he said, "Let not the Lord be angry, and I will speak but once more: Suppose ten should be found there?"

And He said, "I will not destroy it for the sake of ten." 33 So the Lord went His way as soon as He had finished speaking with Abraham; and Abraham returned to his place.

This passage sets a precedent that God will not decree apocalyptic judgement on the righteous with the wicked. It also provides us with part of the reason why God allows the Antichrist to accomplish his aims and murder every Christian on the earth.

Revelation 6 "Number" Reference

It is no coincidence God's response in Revelation 6:11. He tells the martyrs who cry for vengeance on those who murdered them that, "*they should rest a little while longer, until both the number of their fellow servants and their brethren, who would be killed as they were, was completed.*" We immediately see its relation to Genesis 18: 16-33 The number God refers to in Revelation six is the final number of those remaining righteous persons. This needs to be completed before God can rain down on the earth the most apocalyptic of His judgements.

8
1260 AND 1290 DAYS

Revelation 12 and the book of Daniel make it clear that the Antichrist's campaign against the believers will be 1260 days. At the end of the 1260th day the last Christian is murdered. They will understand that within those days they will be no more. The not knowing the day or hour not only does not apply to them, but Scripture lets them know the maximum number of the days of their life. Evangelicals have misused "not knowing the day or hour" to apply to the entire Tribulation.

Ten Days of Tribulation

It should also be noted that Jesus worded *"deliver you up to tribulation and kill you"* and it might be a reference to the ten days of tribulation of Revelation 2:10, meaning that there might be a process the person goes through before they are murdered, and it can involve torture. Jesus instructs in Revelation 2:10, "*Be faithful until death, and I will give you the crown of life.*"

Antichrist Murders Each and Every Christian

Revelation 12: 1-6 makes the 1260 days of persecution very clear. From reading the other passages in the previous chapter we learn that the Antichrist accomplishes his aims and crushes them completely. The passage reads:

12 Now a great sign appeared in heaven: a woman clothed with the sun, with the moon under her feet, and on her head a garland of twelve stars. 2 Then being with child, she cried out in labor and in pain to give birth.

3 And another sign appeared in heaven: behold, a great, fiery red dragon having seven heads and ten horns, and seven diadems on his heads. 4 His tail drew a third of the stars of heaven and threw them to the earth. And the dragon stood before the woman who was ready to give birth, to devour her Child as soon as it was born.

5 She bore a male Child who was to rule all nations with a rod of iron. And her Child was caught up to God and His throne. 6 Then the woman fled into the wilderness, where she has a place prepared by God, that they should feed her there one thousand two hundred and sixty days.

In line with believers not suffering God's judgements, in this wilderness God will miraculously provide food for them. Essentially their tribulation will come from persecution from the Antichrist.

The Two Witnesses

The two witnesses minister during these 1260 days. Revelation 11 records:

11 Now after the three-and-a-half days the breath of life from God entered them, and they stood on their feet, and great fear fell on those who saw them. 12 And they heard a loud voice from heaven saying to them, "Come up here." And they ascended to heaven in a cloud, and their enemies saw them. 13 In the same hour there was a great earthquake, and a tenth of the city fell. In the earthquake seven thousand people were killed, and the rest were afraid and gave glory to the God of heaven.

Most likely the witnesses are resurrected out on the 1260th day, when the final believer is martyred, as well in preparation for the final woe, which the Bible states after that event comes quickly.

The Number of Days to the End

The book of Daniel reiterates the number of days until the end of their lives on earth and it corresponds to Revelation 12. Daniel 12:7-11 reads:

7 Then I heard the man clothed in linen, who was above the waters of the river, when he held up his right hand and his left hand to heaven, and swore by Him who lives forever, that it shall be for a time, times, and half a time; and when the power of the holy people has been completely shattered, all these things shall be finished.

8 Although I heard, I did not understand. Then I said, "My lord, what shall be the end of these things?"

9 And he said, "Go your way, Daniel, for the words are closed up and sealed till the time of the end. 10 Many shall be purified, made white, and refined, but the wicked shall do wickedly; and none of the wicked shall understand, but the wise shall understand.

11 "And from the time that the daily sacrifice is taken away, and the abomination of desolation is set up, there shall be one thousand two hundred and ninety days. 12 Blessed is he who waits and comes to the one thousand three hundred and thirty-five days.

Moreover, there cannot be a Rapture of alive Christians at the end of the Tribulation. They know the number of days for their life including the number till the end of the world, which are 1290 days.

1290 Days

The 1290 days are the days given until the second coming of Jesus and the final pummeling of the earth. The number starts from the abomination of desolation. I have written how in the final 30 days of the Earth are the greatest and worst of the Revelation judgements reserved for when the last believer is martyred.

Daniel 12:10 states: … *"From the time that the daily sacrifices is taken away and the abomination is set up, there shall be one thousand two hundred and ninety days."*

Revelation 15: 1-4 makes this clear:

15 Then I saw another sign in heaven, great and

marvelous: seven angels having the seven last plagues, for in them the wrath of God is complete.

2 And I saw something like a sea of glass mingled with fire, and those who have the victory over the beast, over his image and over his mark and over the number of his name, standing on the sea of glass, having harps of God. 3 They sing the song of Moses, the servant of God, and the song of the Lamb, saying:

"Great and marvelous are Your works,
Lord God Almighty!
Just and true are Your ways,
O King of the saints!
4 Who shall not fear You, O Lord, and glorify Your name?
For You alone are holy.
For all nations shall come and worship before You,
For Your judgments have been manifested."

The Unleashing of the Bowl Judgements

This passage makes it clear that as the seven angels are about to unleash the seven bowl judgements, the martyred saints are all gathered, and their number has been completed. Again, this means that there is not one righteous person left on the Earth. Therefore, God now allows the bowl judgements to be released onto the Earth.

Moreover, proving that the righteous are all now in heaven, when Jesus returns riding His white horse, an army of the Saints is already with Him. The 1335 days might refer to after the great white throne judgement when the rewards are given.

The gathering of the elect recorded in Matthrew 24:31 and Revelation 11:15, refers to the gathering of the bodies of the Tribulation Saints. In Revelation 6, we see that their souls are underneath the alter and when Jesus appears on the earth at the Second coming, and there is the final third resurrection of the First Resurrection. The First Resurrection is completed. Each one Jesus needed to physically be present.

9
SEALING OF THE 144 THOUSAND

Revelation 7: 1 describes,*" After these things I saw four angels standing at the four corners of the earth, holding the four winds of the earth, that the wind should not blow on the earth, on the sea, or on any tree.* "The winds are held back in a stilling. John Dodgson of Phys.org reported in an article in 2017 titled, "The Stilling: global wind speeds slowing since 1960," that winds are slowing. He called the phenomena a stilling. This is similar to what the Bible describes as taking place while the 144 thousand are sealed. Simultaneously at the end of this event, the angels instantly release the winds and at this moment the troops are descending upon Israel as a cloud. Therefore, the stilling and the sealing of the 144 thousand takes place at the very final hours or moments of the Gentile Church age while the coalition troops are in route to Israel.

Releasing of the Winds

Once the final witness has been sealed, the four angels release the winds. Simultaneously the great earthquake takes place and signifies the end of the Gentile Church age. At the timing of the earthquake flooding rain, great hail, fire and brimstone along with the other predicted cataclysmic natural events occur. The believers are raptured out of the earth at this moment.

Ezekiel 38: 21-22 records, *" I will call for a sword against Gog throughout all My mountains," says the Lord GOD. "Every man's sword will be against his brother. 22 And I will bring him to judgment with pestilence and bloodshed; I will rain down on him, on his troops, and on the many peoples who are with him, flooding rain, great hailstones, fire, and brimstone."*

Events in Nature Accompany God's Actions

Several times in the Scriptures we see that when God works in mighty ways, events in nature occur. Around the throne room are thunders and lightening. Other examples in the Bible are the parting of the Red Sea, the earth swallowing the men of Korah, and the destruction of the earth by the flood. We can also add the Rapture of the Gentile church to this list. It will appear as if certain people just vaporized simultaneously with the earthquake, flooding rain, great hailstones, fire, and brimstone.

Brimstone is sulfur. Scientists theorize that Sodom and Gomorrah's destruction resulted from a massive meteor explosion above the earth. A similar one occurred in Russia over 100 years ago.

In addition to the fire and brimstone God will send fire on the coastlands, which indicates extreme heat causing fires. Ezekiel 39:6 predicts, *"And I will send fire on Magog and on those who live in security in the coastlands."* All these catastrophic events will take place simultaneous with the Rapture.

End of the Gentile Church

Once God shows Himself to the nations, this event marks the end of the Gentile

Church. It also ushers in the Tribulation and the 70th week of Daniel.

In the Bible, we see a pattern of evens at the end of each dispensation and beginning of a new one. When Jesus died on the cross, the law officially ended when the veil of the Temple was torn in two. The book of Matthew 27:51 records at the moment of Jesus's death," *Then, behold, the veil of the temple was torn in two from top to bottom; and the earth quaked, and the rocks were split.* "The sun also darkened on that day, which is recorded in three of the Gospels.

Significance of Earthquake

At the death of Jesus and the end of the law, notice the events that occurred in nature particularly the earthquake. In the throne room of God, we see that from His seat emits thunders and lightening's and earthquakes. When God acts forces of nature accompany His actions. In addition, these events are significant.

This cataclysmic earthquake is in line with the one at Jesus's death that ended the law but this quake ends the era of the Gentiles and ushers in the 70th week of the Jews. This confirms the switch in dispensations or time periods. Paul confirms in Romans 11:25, *"For I do not desire, brethren, that you should be ignorant of this mystery, lest you should be wise in your own opinion, that blindness in part has happened to Israel until the fullness of the Gentiles has come in."* The earthquake occurs marking the completion of the number of Saints from the Gentile age saved. In addition, the turning point from the grafted of the Gentiles to the Jews.

God miraculously defeats the massive Ezekiel 38 coalition. He in part accomplishes this through issuing the catastrophic weather that accompanies the earthquake. This will be so great it will destroy the Al-Aqsa Mosque. Along with the strength of this earthquake and its predicted aftermath, the Rapture occurs simultaneously taking out those of the Gentile Church age that are alive to be caught up in the clouds. In addition, all of the dead in Christ's bodies will rise and be joined to their spirits as this is the second of the First Resurrection and can only occur with Jesus present.

This Verse Aligns With Revelation 6

As evidence that this battle begins the Tribulation, we see Ezekiel 38:21 compares with details given in Revelation 6:3. Ezekiel 38:21 states, *"…Every man's sword will be against his brother."* This lines with the four horsemen prediction in Revelation 6:3. It reads: *"When he opened the second seal, I heard the second living creature saying. Come and see, Another horse fiery red went out And it was granted to the one who sat on it to take pace from the earth, and that people should kill one another and there was given to him a great sword."* This killing of one another indicates that the Tribulation season has now started, although it officially begins with the signing of the Antichrist's treaty.

The God of Israel is Back

Another key passage that pinpoints the start of the final season is the statement recorded in Ezekiel 38:23, *"Thus I will magnify Myself and sanctify Myself, and I will be known in the eyes of many nations. Then they shall know that I am the LORD.'"*

Another words, make no mistake, the God of Israel is back fighting on behalf of Israel, as in the days of the children of Israel's early history. Through this event He reappears. The transition, turning point or prelude of the 70th week has begun.

The final passage further predicts and affirms that this event begins the final dispensation and God returning to Israel. God calls Himself; *"The Holy One in Israel"* and God makes Himself known to the Israelites via the same miraculous acts as in their early history and the nation turns to Him. The age of the Gentile Church has ended. This is affirmed several times as we read on:

"Then they shall know that I am the LORD. 7 So I will make My holy name known in the midst of My people Israel, and I will not let them profane My holy name anymore. Then the nations shall know that I am the LORD, the Holy One in Israel. 8 Surely it is coming, and it shall be done," says the Lord GOD. "This is the day of which I have spoken."

God's Word in Israel From This Day Forward.

In the following passages God clarifies the beginning of the new dispensation, which is the prelude to the earth's final seven years, and it clearly is a time for Israel, which matches the 70th week of Jeremiah the prophet. The message cannot be any clearer than in this final passage.

Ezekiel 39: 21-22 affirms: *"I will set My glory among the nations; all the nations shall see My judgment which I have executed, and My hand which I have laid on them. 22 So the house of Israel shall know that I am the LORD their God from that day forward.*

While the rest of the passage elaborates Ezekiel 39: 29 clearly affirms: And I will not hide My face from them anymore; for I shall have poured out My Spirit on the house of Israel,' says the Lord GOD."

In the pouring of the Spirit, the veil or blindness that the apostle Paul talks about has been lifted. The Spirit will help them in the days and horrific trials to come. Meanwhile the 144 thousand begin their evangelism, witness and more.

10
THE RAPTURE & ITS AFTERMATH

In John's vision on the Isle of Patmos, he saw an innumerable multitude of people dressed in white robes, praising God. Revelation 7:9- The elder looked at John and asked who these people were arrayed in white robes and where did they come from.

This was a rhetorical question posed to John and he answers, "*Sir you know.*" The vocal question is used to emphasize the point.

The elder continued: *'These are the ones who come out of the great Tribulation, and washed their robes, and made them white in the blood of the Lamb, Therefore, they are before the throne of God, and serve*

Him day and night in His temple. And He who sits on the throne will dwell among them." Christians will come out of the Tribulation. The blood of Jesus Christ makes them perfect in God's sight.

More on the Phrase "Come Out"

Notice the word "come out" is used, not came out, indicating present tense. The word in the Geek for "come" is erchomai. According to Blue letter Bible's Greek Lexicon the word is a "Middle voice of a primary verb (used only in the present and imperfect tenses..."

The word means:

to come, of persons, to come from one place to another, and used both of persons arriving and of those returning, to appear, make one's appearance, come before the public metaph. to come into being, arise, come forth, show itself, find place or influence, be established, become known, to come (fall) into or unto, to go, to follow one.

 The word "come out summaries the Rapture teaching. Hence believers will instantly meet with Christ in the air and come out of the great Tribulation.

The Rapture

When the final 144th witness is sealed, the Rapture occurs. 1 Thessalonians 4:13-18 confirms:

13 But I would not have you to be ignorant, brethren, concerning them which are asleep, that ye sorrow not, even as others which have no hope.

14 For if we believe that Jesus died and rose again, even so them also which sleep in Jesus will God bring with him.

15 For this we say unto you by the word of the Lord, that we which are alive and remain unto the coming of the Lord shall not prevent them which are asleep.

16 For the Lord himself shall descend from heaven with a shout, with the voice of the archangel, and with the trump of God: and the dead in Christ shall rise first:

17 Then we which are alive and remain shall be caught up together with them in the clouds, to meet the Lord in the air: and so shall we ever be with the Lord.

18 Wherefore comfort one another with these words.

The Rapture's Aftermath

The thief reference depicts Jesus's role in the Rapture. In the Rapture. Jesus comes when we are unaware, and He takes those of us who are His and takes us out of the world. And it is as if we are literally stolen from the world. Simultaneous with the extraordinary weather events brought on in the Ezekiel 38 war we will appear to vaporize or disappear.

Clothing Left Behind

Based on the descriptions of Jesus's burial wraps that covered his body like a garment that were left behind when He resurrected, in addition to Elijah's mantle, it will be the same for believers raptured. Gold teeth, jewelry, prosthetics, metal parts, stents etc. will be left behind. This will make it seem as if there was an atmospheric event that occurred.

Not an Obvious Christian Event

Remember when the Rapture happens it will not be so obvious that Christians were removed. There are going to be those who many would think are Christians who will not disappear. This includes mega church pastors. Individuals one would not think have accepted Christ will be missing. Then there is also the question of babies and toddlers. But Joel 3:3 mentions children during the Tribulation. The verse gives a glimpse of the immorality of that time and states, "And they have cast lots for my people, and have given a boy for a harlot, and sold a girl for wine, that they might drink." There are areas of unknowns when it comes to the Rapture. Some have also asked about their pets. These are all good questions. But the answers we will not know.

Disappearances in History

There were times in history when people vanished. The Bermuda Triangle has had a disappearance of 50 ships and 20 airplanes in a 50-year period. Freaky was flight 19 on Dec 5, 1945. Flight 19, and a squadron of five U.S. Navy torpedo bombers, vanished into thin air during a routine training exercise, during peacetime.

Before losing radio contact off the coast of southern Florida, Flight 19's flight leader was heard saying, "Everything looks strange, even the ocean," and "we are entering white water, nothing seems right." The aircraft and 14 crew members were never found, and even stranger, the search and rescue aircraft with 13 men sent to locate the missing planes disappeared as well.

Tungusta Explosion

Another odd natural disaster was the Tungusta event in Russia. A powerful explosion occurred on June 30 in 1908. Over 1000 reports and papers later and scientists are still not in agreement to the cause. Some speculated that it was made by the air burst of a large meteoroid or comet. They can't agree because if one happens it causes events that did not take place and if a comet occurred there should have been other evidence. So no agreed on what the exact cause was because this occurrence was so strange it does not fit entirely either theory. They figure this took place about three to six miles above the Earth's surface.

Different studies have yielded varying estimates of the object's size, in the order of 330 feet. It is the largest impact event on or near Earth recorded in history. The Tunguska explosion knocked down about 80 million trees over an area covering 830 miles. It is estimated that the shock from the blast would have measured 5.0 on the Richter scale. This type of explosion could destroy a large metropolitan area and was about 1,000 times more powerful than the atomic bomb dropped on Hiroshima.

Witnesses recorded seeing a bluish light, nearly as bright as the Sun moving across the sky. As well as a flash and a sound like artillery fire. The sounds were accompanied by shock waves that knocked people off their feet and broke windows hundreds of miles away.

So it will be with the Rapture, it will occur along with the Ezekiel 38 apocalyptic events in nature that defeat the coalition army against Israel. Only in the event people worldwide will disappear.

Possible Explanations

Scientists will come up with explanations of strange weather phenomena to explain the disappearance. Another possibility is to blame a secret Russian offensive such as in the case of the alleged microwave weapon which debilitated CIA agents who reported constant migraines and vertigo among other symptoms. Only they will claim this was intended to accompany the invasion but went awry.

The Russian Arab armies who went to fight the Ezekiel 38 war will not have disappeared, so they will have a theory about the epicenter of the quake emitting waves that vaporized individuals with a certain blood type, or who ate a certain food, etc.

Others will blame the Chinese. Not to mention the conspiracy theorists who will claim it was a secret covert attack to decrease the population. There will also be those who will claim aliens took them but although with belongings left behind, this will be a hard to believe theory.

The Antichrist Will Use It

The Antichrist will use the Rapture to further his agenda in pushing man made climate change with him and his laws as the solution. If the theory prevails that this was a secret weapon, he will champion finding the enemy. Most likely the cause will be attributed to extreme weather around the predicted weather event that fulfilled prophecy. Moreover, the reason for the mystery of the disappearance of people will take from God's victory in Israel for the rest of the world.

For the unrighteous, the apocalyptic natural disasters that defeated the Ezekiel 38-39 army, they will feel fits into the extreme weather of the day. While a prelude to the Tribulation, it marks that the Tribulation has nearly begun, all that will await is the Antichrist's agreement and his Covenant of Death with Israel guaranteeing the nation peace.

God's Promise

Although Bible prophecy presents frightening truths to the reader, its message is not entirely one of doom and gloom. As you read in this book believers in Jesus Christ will be Raptured and will not go through the Tribulation or have to live under the dictatorship of the Antichrist. This is a great hope for those of us living in these end times.

If you know Jesus as your personal savior, God will take you out of the world in the Rapture just before it begins. God provides us a way out. But, if you do not know Jesus as your personal Savior and if He is not Lord of your life, you will remain behind.

God's gift of eternal life with Christ is simple to obtain, but few will take it. All men are sinners. Sin is anything that we say or do that does not bring glory to God. God is righteous, and the slightest sin within us makes us unrighteous in His sight. There is nothing in and of ourselves that we can do to obtain the favor of God. Isaiah 64:6 states: *"And all our righteousness are like filthy rags."* God will not even accept one into heaven for his good works. Salvation is by faith alone. Ephesians 2:8-9 tells us: *"For by grace you have been saved through faith; and that not of yourselves: it is the gift of God: not of works lest anyone should boast."*

But Romans 10:13 promises, *"For whoever calls upon the name of the Lord shall be saved."* God promises eternal life to anyone who accepts Jesus Christ as his personal savior. John 5:24 states:

"Most assuredly, I say to you, He who hears My word, and believes in Him who sent Me, has everlasting life, and shall not come into judgment; but has passed from death into life."

Insuring You Will Be Raptured

If you want to be sure that you are saved and that heaven will be your home, and that Jesus will keep you too from the hour of trial that is coming on the whole Earth, and from the Antichrist, pray this simple sinner's prayer and mean it with all of your heart and call upon the name of Jesus: *"Oh God, be merciful to me as a sinner, I believe that Jesus died for my sins, and trust Jesus as my Lord and Savior. Thank you, Lord Jesus, for saving me."* Romans 10:13 affirms, *"For "whoever calls on the name of the Lord shall be saved."* It is as simple as calling upon His name.

ABOUT THE AUTHOR

Erika Grey, author, Bible scholar, eschatologist, commentator, and journalist has been a born-again Christian for over 40 years. She has written numerous books and articles on Bible Prophecy and made contributions in helping to decode the more difficult forecasts. She has spoken on numerous radio stations including Coast to Coast. Erika hosts the Prophecy Talk podcast and YouTube Channel.

This book is one of a series of short books by Erika Grey intended to be quick reads with important information. Be sure to check out Erika's other titles at www.erikagrey.com.